Where Are the Monkeys?

Katie Sharp
Illustrated by Jane Dippold

Rigby

Grandma, Joni, and Clay went to the zoo.

"I want to see the monkeys," said Clay.

"Me, too!" said Joni.

"Where are they?" asked Grandma.

"We don't know," said Joni and Clay.

Grandma said, "We need
a map."

"Why do we need a map?" asked Joni.

"A map will tell us where the monkeys are,"
said Grandma.

4

"Don't maps have states?"
asked Joni.

"Some maps have states," said Grandma.
"Maps can help us find a lot of things."

MAPS

WOMEN FOOD

MEN GIFTS

7

"I see a monkey!" said Clay.

"There is a snake, an elephant, a lion, and a giraffe, too!" said Joni.

"We see them all," said Clay.

"Why is this box on the map?" asked Clay.

"It helps us understand the map,"
said Grandma.
"This box shows us where to find
things to eat and buy.
It also shows us where the bathrooms are."

"How do we get to the monkeys?"
asked Clay.

"Look at the map to see
where we are," said Grandma.

"Here we are," said Joni.

"How do we get to the monkeys?"
asked Grandma.

"This way!" said Clay.

"We can see the snakes, too," said Joni.

"Now we see," said Joni and Clay.
"Maps are not just for states.
Maps are for many things!"